PERSEVERANCE

The Power
Beneath
The
Surface

Cynthia Rembert James

Book Design and Layout by Claire A. Henry, BeDazzled Books

Printed in the USA

ISBN 978-0-9760536-9-9
BeDazzled Books
P.O. Box 853
Decatur, GA 30031

Dedication

This book is dedicated to those women closest in my life. My mother Thelma Rembert who gave me a love for the Scriptures, and daughters Nancy and Bre whose lives are so full of promise and giftedness. Special thanks to Shirley Payne for her transcription and to Claire Henry for her willingness to edit and escort this project to completion. A special recognition is in order for all the women in Scripture with whom I feel a kinship as they open their hearts and their lives through the peephole of the text.

Contents

Preface……………………………………...………..7

On the Threshold………………………..…….....11

Rizpah……………………..……...…………..……..39

Miracle in a Miracle……………….…..…………71

Preface

Readers are invited to actively engage their imaginative skills and the author's learning curve while gaining a new perspective on the underlying dynamics in the lives of three women. It is not shocking to anyone when the biblical narratives are sometimes abruptly interrupted with assertions from the author's own life or comparisons to contemporary experiences for women. The sermons were shortened and presented here in hopes of being useful to the academic process of listening to the text and querying the text until the secrets, thoughts and would-be conversations of the characters are revealed. It is believed that this exercise is essential to the development of seminary students and women who may be challenged to present the stories of Biblical women from a womanist perspective.

There is no intent to offer a model for sermon development especially since this material has been shortened from its original presentation and is being offered in a context which was never a part of its originally intended use over twenty years ago. It is always a risky venture to assume that one has some thoughts worth sharing. However, the benefit to be gained from embracing both the pain and the life lessons of these three Biblical Women helps to overcome the writer's embarrassment of being judged by a singular work.

The lines are intentionally blurred in each narrative to give readers a liberty in making contemporary applications. For example, in "On the Threshold," the Levite's concubine, despite her limited rights as a secondary legal wife, is denied access into the male world of friendship and hospitality. As the story progresses, the concubine becomes increasingly invisible to the point where she is both emotionally and physically dismembered.

Women who serve as caregivers are invited to courageously take note of the people and situations that punctuate their lives. The feeble efforts of the Levite's concubine to be self-asserting (i.e. the narrative ends with her on the threshold reaching for the door) are noted and applauded despite the fact that it is too little, and too late to save her from her demise. This woman's cruel end is used as a rally cry to call the Israelites to a unified war.

The question is when will we as women become self-determining enough to insist on having our voices heard. This is not an angry text but one that challenges men and women to open their eyes to any form of de-humanizing abuse and misuse. Finally, it is suggested that preaching women and any student of the Scripture stands to benefit from the postulated metaphor in this reading.

The second narrative is about another concubine, Rizpah, who refuses to be silenced and who through her courageous and faith filled watch over the dead sons of Saul, makes her point to the small and to the great. Rizpah is a powerful metaphor for the church, which needs to heed an increasingly more desperate call to become defenders of social justice.

The blurred boundaries in this narrative compare the literal hanging of seven of Saul's sons to the overwhelming denial, and delays men, particularly ethnic minority men, experience in becoming economically independent. Saul's sons who were hung on a cross are compared to the visible idleness of men (sons) hanging on corners hoping to get work for the day.

The absence of support for Rizpah and for the Levite's concubine makes an argument for the need to connect with other humans. The self-centeredness, greed, and obvious indifference of the community to the person with less social status are a particularly poignant feature of both texts. In fact, in each narrative there are persons who are excluded from the hospitality and good graces of a supportive community.

In the final narrative, the lines are again blurred to allow the reader to visualize an imagined connection between the dying 12-year-old girl and the woman with the issue of blood. A sharper focus offers possibilities for finding the dreams, and ambitions of a dying girl lodged in the overly busy and demanding lives of adult women. There is hope for the woman and hope for the child who is critically ill but not past the point of renewal. The full text employed a series of childhood nursery rhymes to kindle memories of inhibition-free childhood days.

On the surface, the three narratives appear to offer a slightly different twist to each text. Actually, the writer is filtering each text through her own conceptual lens as a psychologist and Christian lecturer. Most importantly, there is an extraordinary blending of actual Scripture with fictive conversations and thoughts of the characters not presented in canonized scripture. The reader will find a distillation of 30 years of wisdom and biblical insight in an unforgettable expression of a womanist worldview.

On The Threshold

*Is There Enough of You
To Go Around?*

PRAYER

Eternal God, help us not to be so enamored with our own images. Help us not to fall in love with ourselves. Help us not to be so moved and impressed with our outer appearances and our experiences that they become prisons for us. We celebrate because you expose our weakness. You expose our failures. You publicly expose our brokenness. Help us now not to feed on the subtle poison of our pretenses. Release us from cover-ups and from spiritual cosmetics so that we can be free. Hunt us down, and by some infinitely merciful stroke of your hand, speak to our heart. Let the poison of our pain become our cure. What we have seen to this day as being horrible, show it to us now as healing. Force our lifelong illusions to die and meet us on the threshold of your love. Amen.

Introduction

God never intended to create us, to work with us, to mold us, and to bring us to a place where we would just die and be destroyed. Many of us have dreams and ambitions that have gotten lost in the shuffle. They have been buried in the shuffle between pinning diapers and going to appointment after appointment. Our visions have been glossed over and hidden. Let us walk through the Word of God, and let the Lord minister to our hearts concerning our need to be whole.

Often, our wholeness is related to our brokenness, and it is the joining that comes from healing our broken and severed condition that makes us whole. Sometimes I feel as if there is not enough of me to go around. Children pull, spouses press, jobs ask for volunteers, hospitals want people to come and work, mission fields are looking for harvesters, the Scouts need a leader; everybody wants something. Sometimes there are just not enough pieces of me to go around.

Is there enough of you to go around? Do you sometimes feel fragmented and broken as though pieces of you are being served to so many needy people?

On the Threshold

Is There Enough of You To Go Around?

I invite your attention to the Word of God, as it is recorded in Judges, the 19th chapter, beginning with verse 1:

> *In those days Israel had no king.*
> *Now a Levite who lived in a remote area in the hill country of Ephraim took a concubine from Bethlehem in Judah. ² But she was unfaithful to him. She left him and went back to her father's house in Bethlehem, Judah. After she had been there four months ⁴ His father-in-law, the girl's father, prevailed upon him to stay; so he remained with him three days, eating and drinking, and sleeping there.*
> *⁸ On the morning of the fifth day, when he rose to go, the girl's father said, "Refresh yourself. Wait till afternoon!" So the two of them ate together.*
> *¹⁰ But, unwilling to stay another night, the man left and went toward Jebus (that is, Jerusalem), with his two saddled donkeys and his concubine.*
> *¹² His master replied, "No. We won't go into an alien city, whose people are not Israelites. We will go on to Gibeah." ¹⁶ That evening an old man from the hill country of Ephraim, who was living in Gibeah (the men of the place were Benjamites), came in from his work in the fields.*
> *¹⁷ When he looked and saw the traveler in the city square, the old man asked, "Where are you going? Where did you come from?"*

²⁰ "You are welcome at my house," the old man said. "Let me supply whatever you need. Only don't spend the night in the square." ²² While they were enjoying themselves, some of the wicked men of the city surrounded the house. Pounding on the door, they shouted to the old man who owned the house, "Bring out the man who came to your house so we can have sex with him."

²³ The owner of the house went outside and said to them, "No, my friends, don't be so vile. Since this man is my guest, don't do this disgraceful thing. ²⁴ Look, here is my virgin daughter, and his concubine. I will bring them out to you now, and you can use them and do to them whatever you wish. But to this man, don't do such a disgraceful thing."

²⁵ But the men would not listen to him. So the man took his concubine and sent her outside to them, and they raped her and abused her throughout the night, and at dawn they let her go. ²⁶ At daybreak the woman went back to the house where her master was staying, fell down at the door and lay there until daylight.

²⁷ When her master got up in the morning and opened the door of the house and stepped out to continue on his way, there lay his concubine, fallen in the doorway of the house, with her hands on the threshold. ²⁸ He said to her, "Get up; let's go." But there was no answer. Then the man put her on his donkey and set out for home.

²⁹ When he reached home, he took a knife and cut up his concubine, limb by limb, into twelve parts and sent them into all the areas of Israel. ³⁰ Everyone who saw it said, "Such a thing has never been seen or done, not since the day the

Israelites came up out of Egypt. Think about it! Consider it! Tell us what to do!"

20 Then all the Israelites from Dan to Beersheba and from the land of Gilead came out as one man and assembled before the LORD in Mizpah.

Judges 19:1,3,4,8,10,12,16-17,20-30, 20:1 NIV

A Daughter of Breaking

This is a difficult passage, at best. One that, on the surface, presents extreme violence. It is one that shows aggression. We tend to skip over this passage because, the protagonist, our central character, has not been placed on a pedestal like Deborah, Esther, Ruth, or Naomi. Few of us, are well acquainted with the story of the Levite and his concubine. Nevertheless, I believe that while reading it, we can ask ourselves, "Are there enough pieces of me to go around?"

Let's look at the context in which she lived. The Word says that this happened during a time when Israel had no king. It was a time when every man did what was right in his own eyes.

Our character is a woman with no name: We dare not leave her anonymous. We will not speak of her as though she's homeless or a transient. We must give her a name. What shall we call her? The writer has provided us with few descriptions, but we should not forget her.

It has been suggested that her name should be "Beth," meaning "house," like Bethlehem. This probably emerged because scripture lets us know in verse 1 that she was from Bethlehem in Judah. However, something about "Beth" is inadequate.

On the Threshold

"House" is the operative word in this scripture. The text revolves around images of home. It's about the presence or absence of hospitality. I can relate to that, because I spend so much time in the house and around the house.

We are women who do not curse our identity. We give life, and our energy gives life to the house and makes it a home. Consequently, the underlying theme revolves around the issues of domestic and community life.

Merely to call her "Beth" is somehow too flippant, and inadequate considering her experiences. I thought about "Bathsheba." "Bathsheba" means daughter of the oath. So why not call her "Bathsheba?" No, not "Bathsheba"; "Bathsheber." We'll call her "Bathsheber." "Sheber," meaning "breaking"; "Sheber," meaning "fracturing," as in limb from limb. "Bathsheber" indicates a dashing of dreams and a denial of hope. "Bathsheber"; "Sheber," meaning, angriness or broken -- anguish or brokenness in spirit.

I christen my hurting sister from Judges, the 19th chapter. I give her a name so that she might not remain anonymous and struggle without an identity. Her name will remind us of what happened to her. Her name will remind us of the pain she suffered at the hands of others and the dismemberment by her own husband. Her name will remind us of more than just her trouble but of the breaking of her dreams. What is her name? "Bathsheber." She is a daughter of breaking.

We, too, are daughters of breaking. Some daughters have been broken by divorce, death, abortion, children on drugs, incarcerated loved ones and illness. There are daughters, Bathsheber daughters, everywhere.

We are daughters of breaking: women who feel, women who ache, women who hurt. It does not fit our made-up, composed posture that we would prefer to project.

Let's walk through this passage. First, she is the concubine of the Levite, but this is not a slave category. She is a secondary wife. It is a legal position, as Bilhah was to Jacob. She has a legal status. Her father was referred to as the Levite's father-in-law. She is a woman with a secondary role. It's curious and odd to me that there is no primary wife in this scripture. There is no sisterhood. There is no first lady to protect her, to advise her, and to counsel her. Nevertheless, she is not without rights. She is a concubine who has limited entitlement as part of her secondary role.

The appropriate term for her status is that of a shiflah. A shiflah is a secondary wife of legal status. The KJV states that she played the harlot against her husband; the NIV translation reads that she was unfaithful to him. Further study shows that there is some question about what was the nature of her unfaithfulness. The custom was that secondary wives or shiflahs were to remain in their father's house and not to go with the husband, as did the primary wife. This woman, left her father's house, and went to her husband's house. After a while she left the husband's house and returned to the father's house. Since we already know the end of the story, we know that subsequently she and her husband journeyed to an old man's house. At no time, and in no place, did she ever seem to have the benefits of a home.

Was this woman unfaithful? What was her crime and what was her sin? Was she adulterous? There is nothing to suggest that she was promiscuous. There is nothing in the Word to imply that she went off with some Don Juan or someone that was tall, dark, and handsome, and spoke smooth words to her spirit. Perhaps her unfaithfulness, some have suggested, was that she violated the old tradition and the old custom; leaving the old way of staying with her father.

Did she leave for convenience, or in hope of a better life? Perhaps she was labeled because she lived on the margins of tradition. Knowing the character of the Levite, it is difficult for us to point a finger at her for leaving him.

It remains unclear why she is called unfaithful, but to her credit, she attempts to be self-asserting and demonstrates some autonomy, although limited. Could it be, that this anonymous woman was trying to make her presence felt and her silent voice heard?

The text does not give her any words. She is the central character, but has no speech. She is nameless and silent, yet it is all about her. How many women today only have the voice of others narrating their life story? This is a key source of tension in the text.

We don't know her crime or her sin, nevertheless, we see that she leaves her husband and goes back to her father. The word that's given there in the Hebrew, that describes her going back home, is synonymous with the word "zanah." That means that she got a divorcement from her husband; an unheard of thing to do in a culture where women were the property of men.

She took a step to free herself. She took a step to actualize and perhaps realize her own dreams. Could it be she was just looking for a safe place? This discussion is not an indictment of men or women rather it is intended to spotlight injustice at its worst. There is something much deeper and much richer in the Word than just playing off personalities and the ill treatment between this man and this woman. The text invites us to look deeper and closer in order to explore the realities of abuse and misuse.

The New International Version states her husband followed her in order to persuade her. The literal translation is that he went after her to speak to her heart. Remember that; to speak to her heart. Is it conceivable that he went after her to speak to the woman-ness; the core of her being and her joy? Could he know the real desires of this nameless, voiceless woman? Did he pursue her as an object, or as a person worthy of recognition?

On the Threshold

You and I could tell her that no Levite, no man, no preacher, no girlfriend, no cousin, no mother or father can speak comprehensively to our heart. Only the Lord has the word to bring new life. No wonder the songwriter said, "Speak, to my heart, Lord. If I can hear from you then I'll know what to do -- speak to my heart."

He went after her, supposedly, to speak to her heart. However, in the course of going to her father's house, the Levite and her father engaged in days of eating, drinking, and male bonding. An event that is intended to affirm her being, instead, pushes her further into the background.

It is just the Levite and the father, going back and forth in this kind of male dominance and rivalry. Ultimately, after much jockeying between the two men, they stay a total of five days. During the course of this time we are given no evidence of exchange between the Levite and his concubine.

Women, today, are still running away – desiring to gain the attention of the one who says they love them. Only the love of God can ascribe full significance and security.

Finally, the Levite says, "Well, we must go, even if the day is far spent, we will go from this place and continue our journey." They travel to Jebus. Jebus, or Jerusalem, had foreigners living in it at the time. Consequently, the Levite says, "We're not going to stay here, in Jerusalem. We are not going to stay in this place, because we will not find hospitality. So let's press our way on to Gibeah, where the Benjamites are." It is ironic that the Levite is seeking hospitality; the very thing he fails to extend to his own concubine. The concubine remains a part of his possessions and his chattel. Essentially, she is invisible and a non-entity.

They come to Gibeah, and when they arrive there, no one invites them out of the city square. It was the custom that when travelers came into a city, they would remain in the city square until offered lodging for the night. Hospitality was part of the culture and the custom. However, in this instance, no one offered his or her home.

They wait in the city square, until an old man comes along. The old man is from the same country of Ephraim, as the Levite. The old man says, "I'll extend my hospitality to you. You can come home with me." Does this "you" extend to the two of them or is he only relating to the Levite, who is from his hometown? When they went home with the old man, the men of the city came and began to knock on the door. Sounds like Lot's story, doesn't it?

Are there enough pieces of me to go around?

We are familiar with what it is to live in perverse times. Violence existed both then and now. As believers, we cannot ignore victims of violence. We understand that we cannot close our eyes to abuse.

On the Threshold

The men knock and pound on the door. They say to the old man, "Send out your guest. We want to have our way with him." But, the old man says, "No! No! I have a virgin daughter here. I will send her out or I will send this Levite's concubine out. Do what you want to do with them, but don't bring this disgrace on this man, my guest."

Somehow, even the virgin daughter disappears. She has been offered, but she never really shows up. She is there, but she hasn't risked anything. She has never left her father's home. She has not ventured out or married. She has not acted. She has not tried to be autonomous. She has no history; no experience. She represents the woman who is silent so no one will notice her, yet she also is a victim of abuse.

When you are a virgin daughter, you can escape the criticism. When it's time for a martyr to be pushed out, you manage to escape the pressure. Are there enough pieces of me to go around? The Levite reaches and takes his own concubine, his secondary wife, and pushes her out of the door. The men took her all night and raped her. It is what we would call today gang rape. It's not a new phenomenon. They had their way with her, each man doing what was right in his own eyes.

Now this woman, Bathsheber; what was her crime again? She had dared to act autonomous, whether in leaving her father or in leaving her husband. She had made an effort and exerted some energy and now she must be punished.

The one who she thought would protect her has now become her punisher. The one that she thought would give her hospitality and safety has pushed her out and become her procurer.

What has happened to the Body of Christ? What has happened to the Daughters of Zion? How do we get to be daughters of breaking? Where we thought we would find safety and refuge, we found our names slandered. We found ourselves being talked about. We found ourselves being objectified.

Where we thought we would find a safe haven or a covering, instead some have been exposed and driven away. Even private confessions at the altar have become fodder for telephone calls. When we thought we could escape our past life, we found our past life followed us every time we got up to sing or every time we got up to speak. Who was it that pushed us out? Was it the Levites? (The workers in the temple.)

This woman was pushed out. She became the victim for the whole city; abused, raped, and misused. She became a victim of not only her circumstances but of her husband's insecurity and his fear for himself. She was indeed a daughter of breaking.

The Word says that they had their way with her all night, but when daylight came they disappeared. Had they stayed, there would be a showing of this crime and an uncovering of the deeds that were done. Now, look at the 26th verse. It says, "At daybreak the woman went back to the house." This is all about house. She went from house to house and from home to home. She ended up where her master was spending the night and she fell down at the door and laid there until daybreak. Perhaps still holding out hope for an ounce of hospitality.

I can envision this woman lying there. The Word says when her master got up in the morning and opened the door of the house, (he must have had a good night's rest), he stepped out to continue on his way, and there lay his concubine, <u>fallen in the doorway of the house, with her hands on the threshold</u>. He did not ask her condition or ask her how she felt; he merely said, "Get up and let's go."

Now, I know that this woman must not have been my complexion, because I believe, having lived with a man like that, even if I was on my last leg and gasping for air, I would manage to put a hand on my hip. If I had never been outspoken before, I would have challenged him with my last breath. I would have been like Samson saying, "God, just strengthen me one more time." Nevertheless, after having gone through a whole night of abuse, she was anonymous one more time. With limited breath and energy in her, she pressed her way back to the door, hoping for safety. She was found lying in the doorway, reaching for the threshold. Maybe her hand was reaching for the doorknob.

Maybe she was thinking that, "Surely, if I can just turn the knob, if I can just push this door open, I'm going to find the protection and the provision that I've been looking for." Maybe she began to think that down in her soul.

As Americans and church folk, we look so polished and beautiful. We live so well, but some of us have been gang raped; not by fathers or husbands, but by situations. Some of us have been gang raped by a system that is oblivious to our identity as the daughters of God.

The pain is well hidden beneath heavily powdered noses and designer clothes. One cannot easily tell what havoc life has reeked. Even when the voice is silent, a woman's body language may disclose her history of violent encounters. One has only to note the downward curve of her mouth, and the light that has gone out in her eyes. The message is, she has worked, birthed, nurtured, and ventured; most often without reward.

Even when there is no voice in the mouth, the body still has a voice. The bodies of black women that have labored over stoves, that picked cotton in fields and rode on the back of buses. The bodies that were not given a voice, or a role, but still their bodies cry out, saying, "Are there enough pieces of me to go around? I am being pulled one way, pushed another way, raped by fashion, abused by the media, and not accommodated by those that set the standards of beauty."

We have been molested all night long, from slave ships and selling blocks to factories. We have been molested all night long, our husbands taken from us, our babies stolen from us. We have been gang raped by a country, gang raped by an insensitive church and the mass media. We have been abused, and misused, but, there is still an ounce of energy left. She presses her way, despite all that has happened; despite the barriers of gender. This woman presses her way to get through the threshold.

As I studied this passage, I began to see another analogy. Other women out there have pressed their way. There is a world that has pressed its way to the threshold of the church. We, the church, have been sleeping all night long, singing songs of Zion, resting on the shore, being comfortable in Zion's old ship. There are wounded and lost women, women that need protection, women that need joy and courage.

Are we so comfortable with our illusions and our pretenses, that we cannot hear the knocking at the door? There are women with open hands, from Haiti to Soweto, from Savannah to North Carolina. There are women on the west coast, women in Australia, women in Bosnia, women that are saying, "If I can just make it to the threshold, I know I'll find help. However, there is a church of Levites inside, at rest, distancing themselves. Souls fall on the altar, and we say, "Get up; let's go. Just repeat the sinner's prayer. Get up and let's go," without heart, without teaching, without compassion. "Get up and let's go."

I see a world that is crawling to the threshold. I see a world of women that want to know, "Can I just get in?" Jesus said, "Behold I stand at the door and knock. If you just open it, I will come in and sup with you." (Rev. 3:20)

When there are broken sisters over here and broken sisters over there and women that are willing to show their brokenness, it sends out a rallying cry that it is time for Israel to come together.

This woman has no words, yet, the positioning of her body, the moving from house to house, tells us she is trying to find a place to fit. But if no one else hears, we must be the primary woman. We must be that first wife that sees the need of the secondary wife. We must understand she has legal status in God's eyes. We must understand that all of God's women need to know the liberation of Christ.

We must not be bought out or sold out to false images attributed to marginalized women. We are not competitive. We are not foolish or strange. We are women of God. We are more than that. We are daughters of breaking. I know what it is to raise children alone. Someone else might say, "I know what it is to try to make ends meet." Another is saying, "I know what it is to not compromise my principles. I know what it is to be a widow. I know what it is to be misused. I know what it is not to have an opportunity," daughters of breaking are coming together.

The Levite comes out and puts her on the donkey. He takes her to his home. Thus far, she has been without home or hospitality. When he gets there, he dismembers her, limb by limb. It is gruesome and violent. The reality is our world is full of fragmented and disconnected lives.

And from the days of John the Baptist until now the kingdom of heaven suffereth violence, and the violent take it by force. (Mat 11:12 KJV) He cut her up, limb from limb. After severing her body, the Levite took her limbs and distributed them to the twelve tribes The broken pieces became a rallying cry calling all of Israel to prepare for war. How many more of our sisters and their children must suffer domestic violence, inadequate health care, and substandard education before we rally.

We have a real agenda that exceeds our praise and worship. In fact, we have a divine mandate to fight for those who cannot fight for themselves and to protest until they find their own voice.

We are pulled by competing needs: loving our children, loving our spouses, aiding our parents, working in the church and responding to societal demands. We are slowly being severed, limb from limb. Some energy here, some strength there, some love there, some compassion there, some help there, some creativity here, some cooking, some mending, some baking, some driving, some chauffeuring, some calling, we are being pulled, limb by limb by limb.

The enemy wants to come and make us curse our dismemberment. But I want you to know there is a blessing in our brokenness, and our wholeness is really the result of our being broken. Our wholeness comes because we are being dispersed. When there are broken sisters over here and broken sisters over there and women that are willing to show their brokenness, it sends out a rallying cry that it is time for Israel to come together. It is time for a new level of unity between God's men and women. We need each other. We are all members of one body.

There is integrity and power in admitting and being truthful about having been hurt. The Word of God says that the Lamb was the one that took the Book of Life. He stood, even as He was slain. (Rev. 5:6)

As the Body of Christ, like the lamb, we too must stand as we are slain gaining power from having been hurt, scarred, and broken. The concubine's parts were sent to the tribes of Israel as a petition for retribution. The great commission sends us into the world that through our brokenness, we might bring healing to others.

On the Threshold

We resist the victimization of women, which leads to powerlessness and broken lives. We strongly espouse a spiritual brokenness before the Lord, which empowers us to be vessels of service for the kingdom of God. We want the Word to go out until every man, woman, boy and girl comes into the hospitality of Christ.

The Levite's concubine was broken by neglect because she was never consulted. She was broken by rejection, because she was never received. Only when she was mutilated and scattered did all of the tribes of Israel begin to understand the message. That is why the Word of God says, but he was wounded for our transgressions, he was bruised for our iniquities: the chastisement of our peace was upon him; and with his stripes we are healed. (Isa. 53:5)

Christ our perfect example, rejected of men in his death made a way for all nations to come into the unity of faith. Blessed Jesus, who is the true High Priest! A husbandman who epitomizes hospitality, who stands at the door, and knocks... stands at the door and knocks. If anyone hears my voice and opens the door, I will come in and eat with him, and he with me (Rev. 3:20); the ultimate of hospitality.

The imagined prayer of the concubine: "Lord, I just barely made it to the threshold. I just pressed my way to the doorway. I am out here waiting. I have been through a hard night. I have been, let down, and kept down but, God I made it to the threshold. I'm stretching out. Reaching for home." See how the High Priest of our soul gives us access? He heals our hurt and grants us deliverance. Consequently, we are not angry women, we are worshipping women who made it to the threshold. The threshold means that we are on the brink of breakthrough. A breakthrough is the power to be and to do; to know and to be known.

Questions for Reflection

1. Take a moment and reflect on your brokenness.

2. Have you confessed your brokenness?

3. How has your brokenness become your blessing?

4. Do you see how your testimony can help another sister on her journey to wholeness?

5. Ask god to give you the courage to share your story with someone who needs to hear it.

6. How often do we, like the old man from Ephraim, only extend hospitality to those with whom we share a common background?

RIZPAH

Introduction

L et me share with you about this woman, Rizpah. If I were to talk to you about Ruth or Naomi or Esther or Deborah, then, indeed, you would know her. You would know something about her work, if her name was Miriam or Dorcas or some of the others, but she is a more obscure character in Bible study.

For some of you she may be new, and I have the great privilege of introducing her to you in this writing. But the person I want you to know is not an individual, not one that bears a gender. Very often in Scripture, where there is a physical reality, seemingly, it really is symbolic and parabolic to us, somewhat of a spiritual position or state or entity.

I invite you to look at Rizpah, not as a woman, but view her as the church; not any church, in the sense of some particular or specific denomination. Not a church of one persuasion or worship style, but the Church of God, in its broadest and most general statement; as those who embrace the living God and His Son as their Personal Savior.

Look at Rizpah, not as a word or a name that is familiar to us, like "Karen" or "Susan" or "Jackie". The name, "Rizpah," takes a little bit of remembering and thinking; we have to enunciate it to get it out, but it's a name in Scripture that has come to mean suffering. Let me remind you that Rizpah is not one of those central, famous characters, not one whose name you would expect to see in lights or on billboards.

Let us look at Rizpah, as if we were looking at a painting. She is an obscure character, almost as an afterthought of the artist. She somehow blends in with the context and in the background of the painting. She is not the central theme of the picture. One has to look closely and, upon close examination, begin to see and understand this marvelous character; Rizpah.

RIZPAH

Then there was a famine in the days of David, year after year; and David inquired of the Lord. And the Lord answered, "It is for Saul and for his bloody house, because he slew the Gibeonites. "Wherefore, David said unto the Gibeonites, "What shall I do for you and wherewith shall I make the atonement that ye may bless the inheritance of the Lord?" And the Gibeonites said unto him, "We will have no silver nor gold of Saul nor of his house; neither for us shalt thou kill any man in Israel." And he said, "What ye shall say, that will I do for you." Verse 6: "Let seven men of his sons be delivered unto us and we will hang them up unto the Lord in Gibeah of Saul, whom the Lord did choose." And the king said, "I will give them. Verse 9: And he delivered them into the hands of the Gibeonites, and they hanged them in the hill before the Lord, and they fell, all seven. And they fell all seven together, and were put to death in the days of harvest. In the days of harvest, in the first days, in the beginning of barley harvest. Rizpah, daughter of Aiah, took sackcloth and spread it for her upon the rock. From the beginning of harvest, until water dropped on them out of heaven, and suffered neither the birds in the air to rest on them by day nor the beasts of the field by night.
2 Samuel 21:1-9, KJV.

RIZPAH

Rizpah was not a woman of great wealth. She was not like the Queen of Sheba. Rizpah was not a woman that had diamonds and gold, but Rizpah was a concubine. If one were to review an earlier chapter of the Book of Samuel, one would see that she had been a concubine to Saul. She was not Wife No. 1. It never feels good not to be number one.

Rizpah was not one that, would command attention when she walked into a room. She was not like those beautiful models going down the runways of Paris. She was not like those women that distinguished themselves in formerly, traditional male occupations. Rizpah was a woman of sorrow, a marginal woman, a woman who was obscure, almost invisible. Rizpah was a concubine. Rizpah was not one that came by legal inheritance into a place of position and power.

Her body and her beauty were used as convenience when desired. Nevertheless, there was some affection there. For Rizpah, this woman of sorrow, was the concubine to King Saul. When you read in the Book, you see that Saul died. When one is in that kind of position, of being indentured or almost in the

45

position of being a possession, when the head person moves off the scene the sky falls in, and the bottom drops out.

Saul died and Rizpah was left with nothing. Even though it had not been the most wonderful existence, at least she had a place to lay her head. Even though she did not get the dignity and the respect that she was due, she had a place where she knew she could eat and sleep. Her protection was gone. Rizpah had to wake up one morning and face the stark reality that there was no Saul, and no king that would call her in and let her sit at a table that had the king's food prepared for those who lived in the palace.

Rizpah had to wake up one morning and know she would never be dressed up and dolled up again and given the perfumes and all of the fanfare that went along with palace life. Rizpah had to wake up one morning and wonder, "Where will my next meal come from? And now I've got to find a place to go and I've got to find a place to sleep and I need to know how I'm going to meet the exigencies of tomorrow."

An argument ensued, the one who was supposed to be the agent and the caretaker of Saul's estate laid claim to Rizpah. He and someone else began to fight over her. Picture this, here are people scrapping over ownership of this woman, and while that is going on, David becomes the king.

There has been a famine in the land for three years and, year after year, David wondered,

RIZPAH

"Why is it so dry? Why is there is no rain? What has happened?" I imagine he went through the routines and he went through the general things that one would do. But, finally, at the end of the third year, David said, "I've reached my end with this situation. Something has to change in our land. Something has to change in our city. We are fed up. We cannot handle this dryness.

We cannot handle this distance and the sense that God is not favoring us. It seems as if He has forgotten us. One year was all right, but doesn't God know that our grass is not going to be there in the field? Doesn't He know that the stalls are going to be empty and that the cattle are going to die? Doesn't He know that there won't be any grain in the fields and the corn is going to be dried-up? Doesn't God remember us in our city?"

So, after three years, David said, "Enough of this dryness," and he inquired of the Lord. In other words, he prayed. He asked God, "What's the matter, Lord? I have been doing everything they told me to do. I was trying to please you. Why is there so much trouble? Why is there so much racial violence? Why is there so much animosity? Why are there so many 'isms' that still survive? Why is there such discord? Why aren't our children saved? Why are our men consumed in the streets? Why are our sons murdered? Why are our daughters used? Why are our classrooms violent? Why is our justice system perverted? Where is the rain, God?"

David began to pray and cry out to God. God spoke to him and said, "Listen, David, this is not a situation of your own doing." He said, "This is because of Saul's deeds and Saul's bloody house."

We have to know that some situations are not our creation. We should not judge people and say, "Well, you're having a hard time in your life; you must have backslid. You are experiencing trouble after trouble and storms of trouble; you must not be trusting God. You must not believe God."

You have to get rid of sin. You cannot master sin. You cannot teach sin. You cannot train sin. You have to conquer sin.

Those statements come from the mind of one that has not lived very long and has not drunk deeply from the Well of God. For if we think about it, we will find that some situations, are not of our doing. We did not create them. We never desired them, but we inherited some of our trouble.

You might begin to look around and say, "I don't know where this came from. I never planted the seeds for this fruit. I never intended for this to happen in my household. I never knew this would sit at my table. I never knew I would put a murderer to bed. I never knew I would comb the hair of one that was corrupt.

The Lord spoke to David and said, "This is out of Saul's house." This did not come out of prayer. Hallelujah! This did not come out of holiness. This didn't come out of fasting. This did not come out of walking with God. This did not come out of believing and trusting God. This didn't come out of being God's chosen people, but this came out of Saul's house; his bloody household. So David decided he would make things right. David wanted a quick remedy, as we sometimes do. Let me just do something fast. I am going to go on two 40-day fasts. Let me just do something quick. I am going to pull heaven's glory down and all of its power overnight.

It had been three years and he had not had an insight on what was going on, but David was looking for a quick solution. As he began to see what happened, the Lord spoke to him -- the Lord said, "David, Saul broke the covenant that Israel had with the Gibeonites. The Gibeonites had fooled the Israelites. The five kings had come against Israel, and they tricked them. They tried to make it seem as if they wanted to make an alliance with Israel."

You know when you are doing God's business you have to know how to be compassionate but not have a weak heart. You cannot afford to get blind and foolish and react impulsively. You have to check things out and go to the root of the problem.

So the Gibeonites pulled a trick on Israel and, instead of being eliminated -- because God said, "Eliminate all of them" – they were able to ease in among Israel and get jobs and become part of the economy. They were to carry the water, carry the wood, and serve them. (See Joshua 9)

You have to get rid of sin. You can't master sin. You can't teach sin. You cannot train sin. You have to conquer sin. Therefore, the Gibeonites had the opportunity to assimilate. For some reason, Saul decided to kill the Gibeonites after all. He had broken a promise. Israel had said to them, "We will not slay you. You can just come and work for us, but we are not going to fight you, like we fought the others." The Gibeonites pretended to worship the God of Israel.

Saul broke this covenant. David determined he would make it right. Saul did something wrong and that caused the dryness. David thought, "I am going to get me a quick remedy and I'm going to go fix this thing." He went to the Gibeonites for advice. That was the first problem.

We cannot go to the world that is full of problems for a solution to the world's problems. We cannot go to Satan and ask him how to put him out of business. We cannot go to systems that have failed and become corrupt inside and outside and expect that moving up to the boardroom will put things in order.

David went to the wrong place, looking for answers and solutions. He went to the enemy's camp and said, "How can I please my God?" I don't know about you, but there's nothing the world can tell me about serving God. There is nothing the world can teach me about living holy. Go to the Word of God, get it from the Mouth of God, and have the Breath of God breathe through you. David went on a quick trek and he went to the wrong place. He went to the Gibeonites.

What happens when God's church begins to identify too closely with the world? What happens when they want to make peace with the world? What happens when God's church is under attack and when our communities are under attack and our children are under attack, and we begin to look to the world systems for relief and solutions? I want you to know that God's church has to have a new vision; a vision that reflects His image. God's church has to have an absolute Word from God. We cannot get it from the newspaper or from city hall alone. We should not expect to get a vision from the police academy or the university alone.

David made a mistake. He said to the Gibeonites, What can I do to make peace with you? I know that I didn't do it; that Saul broke the covenant that Israel had and he slew some of the Gibeonites and we promised we'd never kill you. But just tell me what I can do, so we can have peace?"

Maybe, if we could just hang in there past the discrimination and get to their schools and manage to hold our heads up and walk through their universities and carry out a couple of their degrees. Maybe women will see real economic equity. Maybe they will give a few corporate seats to us. Maybe if we can just put some of our culture to the side and put our Christ to the side, we will be accepted.

Maybe if we can begin to talk the world's language and live the world's lifestyle, maybe we will be mainstream. As you look into the Scriptures, you will see that this is not the solution. There is no quick solution, no overnight, snap-it-out remedy. We have to do it God's way. Sadly, David went to the Gibeonites.

When we give that much power to the enemy, when we can't seem to assist our own community, we say, "You tell me what to do with my child. You tell me how to fix my home. You tell me how to repair my shattering marriage. You tell me how to stop our schools from faltering. You tell me how to stop the financial havoc in our community, too many dollars are going out instead of circulating and coming in. When we begin to go to the Gibeonites for help, we are on a suicide mission.

When David began to talk to the Gibeonites, They said, "We don't want your money. We're not impressed with silver and we don't want your gold." Look at Verse 4: *We will have neither silver nor gold of Saul nor of his house, neither for us shalt thou kill any man of Israel.* We don't want an eye for an eye and a tooth for a tooth. No. We want a very specific atonement for having broken that covenant.

RIZPAH

David promised them in the previous verse. He said, "I will make the atonement. What ye shall say, will I do for you." And they answered the king: "The man that consumed us and that devised against us, that we should be destroyed from remaining in any of the coasts of Israel, let seven men of his sons..." In other words, the Gibeonites said, "All right, you want to make up for Saul having broken his promise with us, let seven of Saul's sons" -- seven, being complete; seven, being total, covering every day of the week. They said, "Let seven men of his sons be delivered unto us and we will hang them up unto the Lord in Gibeah of Saul, whom the Lord did choose." And the king said, "I will give them." The Gibeonites said, "Wait a minute. We do not want something general. We definitely don't want money."

We thought it was about economics, but it's not. We thought it was about credentials, but it is not. We thought it was about property and getting a house in another neighborhood, but it is not. We thought it was about being able to get a used luxury car, but it's not about any of that. The Gibeonites said, "Give us seven of Saul's sons."

David, in a foolish moment, wanting a quick relief, said, "I will give them." Our adversary is still asking for our sons more than our stuff.

David spared Mephibosheth, because of his bond and his covenant with Jonathan, who was Mephibosheth's father. Now, I love to preach about Mephibosheth and how he got to come to the King's table, but the Holy Ghost quickened something different in my mind. The one he spared was disabled. The one he spared could never go to battle, could never pick up a weapon and fight the enemy. Similarly, our sons who are disabled by drugs, AIDS, or nearly a lifetime in prison cease to be a threat.

David spared Mephibosheth out of a good motivation, out of a good intention, because of his covenant with Jonathan. However, Mephibosheth could not do the job anyway. Mephibosheth was not the promise of the next generation. Mephibosheth was not the future of the church. Mephibosheth was not the Savior and the deliverer of the communities. Mephibosheth had already been maimed by his nurse.

The king spared Mephibosheth, the son of Jonathan, the son of Saul. That was Saul's grandson, but look at Verse 8: *the king took two sons of Rizpah, the daughter of Aiah, whom she bear unto Saul.* Two of her sons were Saul's children -- Armoni and Mephibosheth. That is another Mephibosheth. And David also took the five sons of Merab, the daughter of Saul.

So, again, here were five more sons who were Saul's children. Two that were mothered by Rizpah and five that were the sons of Saul's daughter. David took these seven sons and delivered them to the Gibeonites, and they hung these seven sons on the gallows from sunup to sundown.

As I drive through streets of Oakland, CA and other urban areas, I don't understand. If I go for a walk at 6:00 or 7:00 a.m., I see some sons hanging on the corner. When I enter or leave the job, I still see some sons hanging on the corner. I see some that don't seem to have any occupation or anything to occupy their minds. They seem to have their wasted gifts and talents. They are sitting on carts outside of stores and sitting with their heads nodding on the park benches or sitting on the curb.

I see sons that don't have any sense of cleanliness. I see sons that are still wearing yesterday's clothes. I see sons talking to people and even cursing at people and there is no enemy anywhere in sight. No matter where I look, seven days a week, twenty-four hours a day, I see the sons of Rizpah hanging. Now, whose sons am I talking about? I am talking about marginal people. I am talking about African-American people. I am talking about Caucasian people. I am talking about Latino. I am talking about Native Americans, who were destroyed without regard for their culture, language, or history.

This thing is too big for one generation. This thing is bigger than one culture. I'm talking about all the sons of disenfranchised people who have been locked out, kicked out and left out. I am talking about how they have hung our sons from Soledad to San Quentin, how they have hung them in Special-Ed classrooms, and unemployment lines.

We need more than a quick solution. When I begin to look at the Word of God, I see the price that Satan is demanding of us is entirely too steep. I am not interested in an assimilated church. I am not interested in an accommodating church, if it is going to take the fruit of our wombs. I am not just talking about male sons, but I'm talking about our children. I am talking about our future.

I suddenly began to understand why God had given this Word to me. Because when our church went through its most recent transition, it was on a Sunday morning that a 14-year-old boy named Imani Butler had been killed in front of church. It was that day that our son was hung, and we made up our mind that it would no longer be lip service. God shifted something down in the depths of our souls. We learned how to get angry at the devil and say, "You will not, you shall not invade and intrude. You will no longer rob our wombs."

David gave away the sons. I know his intentions were good. This is not about a guilt trip. I know he just meant to bring peace to Israel. I know he thought it would remedy the dryness, but the sons of Israel were hanging; all seven of them hanging.

Think what a disgrace. The little children would walk by and they would say, "Is that my future?" The little boys would walk by and say, "Is that all I have to look forward to?" The mothers would walk by and turn their heads in shame and say, "Why did I labor?" The fathers would walk by and their hearts would hurt, but they would hide it, because of their manly appearance. Perhaps they were not callous and indifferent as the world would say; perhaps they were angry inside.

They looked at the hanging sons. Verse 9 states, *They delivered them unto the hand of the enemy, the Gibeonites, and hanged them in the hill. And when they got through hanging them they fell, all together. They, all seven, fell together and they were put to death in the days of harvest.*

Is this harvest time? Is this harvest month? Is death everywhere? If it sounds like a morbid message, it is not. If you think it is oppressing, it is not. No. It is a different kind of rally; a different kind of liberating call. It was during the time when they should have been getting the results and the fruit from the field of seeds that had been planted. It was a false harvest. It was a phony harvest.

Harvest time was a time when there should have been celebration. There should have been gathering in from the fields. Instead of a harvest, there was death. The beginning of barley harvest signaled when the poor man expected to eat. It was when the disenfranchised ought to have his day and everyone else has had their day.

Rizpah, the daughter of Aiah, what did she do? *She took sackcloth and spread it for her upon the rock.* Now, this woman could have been involved in all the festivities of harvest. She could have chosen to say, "Saul is gone. I have to move on. I have to secure another home. I have to find shelter. But Rizpah made a choice not to let the death of the king's sons go unnoticed. She made a volitional, intentional, choice. She was not duped into it. She was not tricked into it.

Rizpah made a decision. She took sackcloth, rather than silk or fine linen. She said instead, "I'll take for myself sackcloth." It reminds me of another Rizpah, because the spirit of Rizpah has nothing to do with gender.

Rizpah has no geographical boundaries. Rizpah is anyone who redeems others and empties their life of self. Rizpah is anybody who had to live on the fringes. There is something about marginality that qualifies one to do a work. When one has to live on the margin one ought to have a special empathy and compassion for human suffering.

I want you to know that God's ministries and His church must be marginal, because we serve a marginal Savior. We serve a God, in the person of Jesus Christ that always had to stay on the fringes. He was not embraced in His hometown. His own homeboys did not understand him. The Pharisees and the Sadducees left him out. They chose to deny His authority, His power, and His position. They lied on Him, cheated, undermined, and plotted against Him.

So, when I get to the tenth verse, my soul gets happy, because I see this is not a woman merely taking sackcloth, but this is a church on the margin that says, "If it were not for the goodness and the grace of God, I would not be here today. If it were not for the everlasting mercy and the loving kindness of God, I would have never discovered that there is victory in my deliverance. If it were not for the amazing grace of God, I would have never learned how to walk the straight and narrow way."

Rizpah kept the vision of the hanging sons before her day and night. When we rise to eat, if our sons are hungry we should not be able to enjoy our meal. When I begin to read, I can't enjoy it, because some of my sons have never learned how to read. When we receive our paychecks we should see our sons unable to find work.

Rizpah had no peace; she had a burden. We must be believers with a burden. That takes sackcloth; a symbol of prayer, fasting and consecration. When everyone else pronounced them dead, I want you to look at the champion, heroic, actions of Rizpah. *She took sackcloth and spread for her upon the rock.* I don't know if she needed the sackcloth to give her warmth when it was cold at night or if she had to use it to keep the heat off her in the glaring sun in the daytime, but whatever it was, her use of sackcloth to symbolized a prayer covering.

She used it as assuredness, a weapon, and a part of the key weaponry in her arsenal. She took the sackcloth and spread it upon the rock. From the beginning of harvest -- she prayed day and night.

The writers and the commentators have speculated there must have been a period of about five months. Now, get a picture of this. We love our loved ones, but we love them to a point, and there is a point where they go further than we are willing to go. We do not go in the grave with them. We go to a certain point and we say, "Precious memories, how they linger." However, Rizpah stayed there, and the bodies began to decay. Nothing lovely about those bodies; they began to rot.

Those bodies must have had a noxious odor. There is nothing sweet smelling about serving the homeless; nothing that is pleasant, nothing that feels good. There is nothing that feels good about laboring with a young woman that has just had her body abused. There is nothing pleasant, soothing, and reaffirming about an incorrigible young person with a chip on his or her shoulder that curses you out when you try to give them a sense of direction; nothing about that is pleasant. Rizpah said, "I'm going to stretch out until the rain comes. I'm going to lie before the Lord until water drops from the sky."

RIZPAH

When you put yourself in that position you will become a victim of criticism. Everybody that walked by probably said to themselves, "What's the matter with Rizpah?" The other concubines may have walked by and said, "Too bad, Honey; you better get over your grief." And somebody else went by and said, "I wouldn't cry over anything dead." Nevertheless, the Word of God says Rizpah spread out on that rock from the beginning of harvest until water dropped on them out of heaven.

At first blush this appeared to be a passive posture. However, we have come to see how it is really a position for warfare. While she was praying and stretching out and exercising faith and believing God, she had to fight. In the daytime the birds came; the vultures. The birds came to eat the seed. It was enough to challenge the seed of faith in Rizpah's heart. She persevered in her love for the sons. It's conceivable that others wanted to tell her she was losing her mind and wasting her time.

Rizpah stayed there as if they were all her children. That is what happens when you begin to stretch out before God. Rizpah modeled care and compassion for those who were not her own.

It is time for the church to understand that those are our sons hanging on the gallows. That was my Stephen and my Edgar and my Reggie that somebody shot down in cold blood on August 31st. It does not matter that they didn't come out of my physical womb, but when I pray, I pray for the born and the unborn children.

Rizpah was a dynamic woman. She lived in Old Testament time, but she had a Twenty-first-century understanding. She had a Twenty-first-century vision. She had a global ministry. She said, "I'll not just reach out to mine, but I'll stay here and I'll wait on God until the rain comes." She said, "I'll pray until jobs come. I will seek God until housing comes. I will stretch out on the rock until relief comes, until health care comes, until security comes." She stayed there, stretched out, from the beginning of barley harvest. She had to hold the sackcloth with one hand. (It reminds me of Nehemiah's army and workers.) She had to use the other hand to fight the vultures.

She said, (look at her spirit), "Haven't you done enough? They have already killed them. They did not give them the honor of a burial; their bodies just laying here on the rock. I could not do anything about it, but I am not going to let the vultures eat them. I am not going let their bodies become a prey for the wild birds."

Maybe I could not help what happened in the mid-Atlantic Ocean, and maybe I can't do anything about the sons that died in slave hellholes. I couldn't do anything about the families split up on auction blocks, or the babies that were ripped out of their mothers' arms, but I am sure I can be a Rizpah in my community.

RIZPAH

She said, "I'm going to stay here and I'm going to fight the birds." Cocaine does not have to take over our cities. Mental illness does not have to take over our communities. Insanity in our homes does not have to take over our families. She said, "I'm going to do something about it."

Every time I get an image of Rizpah stretching out on the rock, my mind goes to another Rizpah that was in the Garden of Gethsemane, saying, "Lord, if it be Thy will, let this cup pass from me." But at the same time saying, "Nevertheless, not my will, but thy will be done." I can see my Rizpah, Jesus, the fullness of God Omnipotent, the Majesty and the Power of all of heaven, stretching out for my salvation; stretching out on Calvary for my deliverance.

I can see Rizpah fighting the vultures out of the air, saying; "Get thee behind me, Satan." Not only did Rizpah fight the birds in the daytime, but also she kept on praying and stretching out on the rock. However, she had to fight the beasts at night. She had to fight and you know what the beasts are? Mental beasts, the anger, the intimidation, the worry, the fear, the low self-esteem, the creeping coldness of feeling a lack of self-worth; those are things that devour.

Rizpah stretched out and fought the birds in the daytime, and the beasts in the nighttime. I can hear her saying, "I don't care how they laugh at me. This is not new to me. I was always the concubine. Therefore, since I am acclimated to marginality, I will just stay on a marginal rock, with a prayer lifted to Yahweh."

The Word of God said she prayed until the rain came. Now the reason this whole thing started is because there was a famine in the land. There was racial animosity in the land. There was enmity of some of God's people in the land. She said, "I'm not going to let go until the Lord moves."

The rain symbolizes the refreshing of God. It symbolized the power of God, coming down like dew drops. It symbolized a revival for the field; a strengthening for the oxen. It symbolized wheat in the fields. It symbolized grain and the corn on the stalks. Rizpah stretched out, with no regard for time.

God is calling for a people and He's calling for a church that is not just looking for its own comfort. God is not looking for a church that is only preoccupied with its own agenda and that only can pray for its own children.

God is looking for a church that can identify many sons on the gallows. God is looking for a church that will stretch out and take a risk on their behalf. Rizpah stretched out until the rains came. She stretched out until relief came. We can stretch out and that's not just shutting in.

Now it is time to know how to keep what we have in God spiritually and how to do warfare simultaneously with the other hand. We need to know how to fight the vultures away and say, "You will do no further violence, no further degradation to our sons. You will not disgrace them or dishonor them anymore. This is where the line stops. We will know how to fight the fierce animals at night." Rizpah represents a church of notable courage, a church that sees no foe as invincible but which, day and night, is unrelenting in prayer.

We need to stay until rain comes. Begin to see in your mind and your heart those that you know personally that you have given up on. Ask the Lord for forgiveness.

Sons and daughters that bought their way into jail, and maybe you said, "let them stay there. They had no business getting there, in the first place." Say, "Oh, God, forgive me. Young people that I discouraged and said, "You'll never be anything. God, forgive me for walking past the gallows and saying, "It isn't my business."

You're not going to go anywhere. You are just like your old daddy; just like your old mama. I don't have any time for you, God, forgive me." We have written off so many sons and daughters.

I know it is unfamiliar territory, to look at the Scriptures that way, but walk with me in an unfamiliar place. We ask God to forgive us for the sins that others have committed. God, forgive me for my part in helping to produce this conscienceless generation. God, forgive me for walking past the gallows and saying, "It isn't my business." God, forgive me for enjoying my coffee and my cake; for being at peace when I put my head on my pillow; for not having the sins invade my dreams and turn them into a nightmare.

God, forgive me for stretching out for me and mine, my four and no more. God, forgive me. Now I am coming to a place where I can identify with Jesus not only as resurrection, but also in the suffering; I'm going to stretch out.

Begin to feel yourself being extended. Begin to experience your thoughts expanding. When you look again you will automatically see new opportunities for work, for service, and to minister.

It is time for us to learn how to grow in the Spirit; how to expand. Our hearts expand first when we begin to include others and a thing called the generation gap disappears. When we submit to a mandate of unity and a new level of oneness, we expand.

Your hurt is my hurt, your task is my task, and your challenge is my challenge. I know I am supposed to love you, support you, and challenge you, and you are to do the same for me. As a church, let us make up our minds to stretch out until God sends relief. I don't care who says it looks dead. I do not care who says there is no hope for our community. I do not care who says it is too late. I defy the lie that says there is "a lost generation." I defy the lie that labels, "Generation X." Rizpah, a viable example of a persevering woman who appeared to be powerless, but who ably drew on her inner strength to restore honor and dignity to the victimized.

Questions for Reflection

1. What marginalized persons are you praying for today?

2. Who have you added to your prayer list as a result of reading this chapter?

3. What will you do to correct the injustices that you see in your community every day?

4. How will you encourage the next generation?

Miracle in A Miracle

What about the children?

PRAYER

Father, we thank you for being so faithful to us. Deliver us from a parade of our flesh. We invite you to manifest your presence and your power. If you were to fully show us yourself, we know, Lord, that we really could not handle it. But do all for us and do as much for us as our frailty can bear. Bless us now from Your Word. Bless us with the fellowship of our sisters and brothers. Then bless us, Lord, with an outpouring of your spirit and an increase in our faith that will lead us to possess more of your will and works. Bless us over and through every inadequacy. We give your name the praise. In the strong name of Jesus. Amen.

Introduction

When we look at ourselves we should be able to see that we are a miracle in miracle. There's one miracle we see when we get through combing our hair and straightening up our jackets and grabbing our purses and trying to match up last year's and last decade's clothes; trying to make them look new. When we have taken care of the children and our spouses and nurtured and loved grandchildren and worked in the house of God. We have prayed, got in the mirror, and encouraged ourselves - that is another miracle. Then, there is another miracle in us that we do not see. The one that walks the floor sometimes, shake our heads sometimes, just has to cry sometimes, cannot really pray, cannot sing a song, but just has to moan sometimes.

There is a miracle on the outside, but in every daughter of Christ, there is a miracle inside of that miracle. The writings in Mark present us with a miracle embedded in a miracle.

PERSEVERANCE

Women of God are learning that we cannot look to the media to encourage ourselves. Our family and friends may forget our birthday, but we can't count on others to encourage us. The spirit of God comes to lift us, to cheer us, and to console us and we become a miracle in a miracle.

Miracle in a Miracle

Mark 5:21 When Jesus had again crossed over by boat to the other side of the lake a large crowd gathered around him while he was by the lake. One of the synagogue rulers named Jairus came there. Seeing Jesus, he fell at His feet and pleaded earnestly with him, My little daughter is dying. Verse 25: And a woman was there who had been subject to bleeding for twelve years. She had suffered a great deal under the care of many doctors and had spent all she had, yet instead of getting better, she grew worse. Verse 30: At once Jesus realized that power had gone out from Him. He turned around in the crowd and asked, "Who touched my clothes?" Verse 32: But Jesus kept looking around to see who had done it. Then the woman, knowing what had happened to her, came and fell at His feet. Verse 34: He said to her, "Daughter, your faith has healed you. Go in peace and be freed from your suffering." While Jesus was still speaking, some men came from the house of Jairus, the synagogue ruler. Your daughter is dead, they said. 'Why bother the teacher anymore? The end of Verse 36: don't be afraid; just believe. Verse 39: "He went in and said to them, 'Why all this commotion and wailing? The child is not dead but asleep. Verse 41: "He took her by the hand and said to her,' Talitha koum!' (which means, 'Little girl, I say to you, getup!'). Little girl, little girl, get up" – A Miracle in a miracle.

This is a Word that is in season. It is a Word that is applicable to God's men and women. It is a Word that is timely for the little children. When

75

Jesus had again crossed over by boat...this was not His first crossing. He had crossed once and now He was repeating it and crossing over again. Therefore, He crossed over again by boat to the other side of the lake.

The Word says a large crowd gathered around Him while He was by the lake. Mark, who was generally concerned about movement and fitting things together in his writings, is letting us know, by the word choice, that this was a repeated journey.

Every now and then, the Lord requires that we go back to some lessons we thought we had learned. Every now and then, things we thought we were delivered from, and had mastered in our flesh, are revisited and He says to us in the still of the night and the early part of the morning, "You're going to cross over again. You're going to go right back where you have been."

He lets us know that, in the spirit, we sometimes have to go back to places we have previously traversed. We have to go back to places and scenes that we thought we had forgotten. We have to go back to conversations that are barely traces in our memory.

We have to go back to feelings of yesterday. We have to cross back again, not because we are trying to belabor the past, or because we do not want to progress and move on. He does not cause us to cross back over because we are fixated with things in our past, but because the

Miracle in a Miracle

Spirit of the Lord will sometimes say to us, "I want you to cross over again." This time, when you go through old familiar territory, begin to see new things; get new perspectives, new insights.

There were two shores on the side of that lake. Anything that has a left has a right. Anything that has a top has a bottom. Anything that has one side, you can count on it having another side. If there is an up, there is a down. If there is an outside, then there is an inside. The Word of God is giving us perspective on the key sides of things, a miracle in a miracle, a dying girl, and a sick woman. There is a miracle on the outside, but wherever there is an outside, there is an inside. Jesus is saying, "Let's cross over again."

He is crossing over to the other side of the lake. Lakes, streams, rivers, oceans, and all of those bodies of water, very often in Scripture, are meant to be symbolic of the tides of our lives. Sometimes the waves are calm, then a storm rises, and after that, there is often peace.

Perhaps He is saying that as we move through life we need to look at both sides. The Gospel of Mark is giving us a sequence of events. The writer makes it obvious that there are two protagonists. There is a dying girl and there is a sick woman. We understand that they appear to be two separate persons. However, there is something intertwining about them, something about them that, as God's women, we can relate to.

I know what it is to be sick. I know what it is to have the concern of loved ones, like Jairus' daughter. Women know the feeling of being isolated and separated because of gender or conditions, like the woman with the issue of blood. We can identify with both the child and the woman. I have always wondered why the Scriptures started with the child and then interrupted the narrative with the woman's issue.

Jesus diverted his attention to the woman and then, as abruptly, takes us right back to the child. What is it saying to us, as women of God and as people of God, about our own growth and halted development? Allow me to suggest to you for a moment that, as I read this passage, after years and years of reading, I want to propose that there is a deeper level on which we can receive from God's Word.

There is more than a gender connection between the child and the woman. There is a reality to their experiences that goes beyond relating to this woman who had medical appointment after medical appointment, until she was tired of going to doctors. It seemed futile to seek any more help from the physicians.

I want to suggest to you that somewhere, perhaps existentially, even though this is a dying girl and a sick woman, there is something similar about their experiences. We are all connected.

Miracle in a Miracle

When I look at you, I see myself. When you look at me, you see yourself. Either I am headed where you are going or you have been where I am. You know what it is to have children. You know what it is to have them leave home. You know what it is to rock the cradle. You know what it is to pray for them when they refuse to come to the house of God, where you weaned them.

When we look at each other, we see ourselves. There is a joining of God's women, like Ruth and Naomi, like Deborah and Sisera's mother and Jael, who was in the tent. It has nothing to do with degrees or status. It has nothing to do with whether you are wearing sackcloth or designer labels. However, God knits something together when he begins to work with His women.

We know that we must be careful where we insert our impressions. Women know that they must be prayerful when they want to see the hand of God move. There is something distinct, as well as something strikingly similar about the girl and the woman. I am going to, not only ask you to look at the two of them in a new way, but also for those of you that are particularly courageous, why not look at the little child that is within - your own miracle in a miracle.

Verse 21 states, A large crowd was gathering around Jesus. While Jesus was by the lake, right there in the midst of the large crowd, one of the synagogue rulers by the name of Jairus approached him. Jairus was one who had the duty of seeing to the order of the service. He was one who was elected by the elders in the congregation. He was one who, although he was the ruler, came to talk to a Ruler.

As a synagogue ruler, he was also called prince of the synagogue; one who was a prince came seeking a Prince. They were distinct, yet they were very much alike. Comparisons can be made between the child and the woman, and the Prince of Peace and Jairus the prince in the house of the Lord.

This man Jairus came and seeing Jesus, he fell at His feet and he honestly began to plead with him and to intervene for his little girl. I wonder had Jairus heard Jesus' words "Suffer the little children to come unto me" and to "forbid them not, for such is the kingdom of heaven." (Matt 19:14)

I wonder had he heard about how Jesus touched the coffin of the widow of Nain's son, and how he had been resurrected. Nevertheless, Jairus, in the face of death, could not find any comfort in the synagogue halls or among his colleagues. We can be so pressured by life until titles and possessions bear little meaning. In these situations, seemingly, only God can reach us. All we want to do is talk to the Son of Man. Jairus was at that place. He was not looking for the high and the mighty. He was not looking for those with great titles and position. But he said,

80

"I have a dying child and I just want to get to Jesus."

He connected with the Lord and began his petition, "My little daughter, my little girl, is dying." He said, "Please come and put your hand on her, so that she can live again." Jesus turned and began to go with him to attend to his dying little girl.

As Jesus turned, the large crowd followed Him and pressed on Him. It is easy for children's issues to get lost in the press. It is easy for little-girl and little-boy agendas to be overlooked in the shuffle of our society.

In the press of unemployment figures, in the press of housing crises and health reform, who is worried about whether or not our children graduate knowing how to read? Who is concerned about a dying child? It is easy to get comfortable with our houses and new cars with gold lettering and forget about the children's issues.

> Wherever there is a dying girl that has been forgotten, it will result in a sick woman.

It is shocking to hear news stories about eight and nine-year-old girls drafted for prostitution in Japan. These innocent children become the new statistic in the rising AIDS epidemic. However, the same pattern is occurring in Johannesburg, Tampa, Florida, Oakland, California and South Central Los

Angeles. It is easy for children's issues to get lost in the press. What about the children?

Women, mothers, have we gotten so glad about our briefcases, business cards and board rooms, that we forget we are the ones that are called to rock the cradle? Are we too cute to wipe the lip that dribbles, to dab the teary eye or to bandage the skinned knee?

What about children's issues? Modern Women of God, what happens to the issues of the dying girls? What happens when we become busy with the things that are all around us? What happens when mama's boyfriend demands more attention and grandmother is too tired to raise another generation?

Tragically, some urban children decide the only way they can get three square meals a day, and clean clothes, is to be locked up in San Quentin. What happens when they think the only way they can get decent dental care, and medical care, is to go to jail? What happens when they think the only way they can be supervised day and night and be parented is when they are a part of the criminal justice system"?

In the decade when women appear to be rising to new heights, what happens to the plea for dying girls and dying boys? What of the dying children that are unable to resist the influence of crack cocaine? What of the dying children that find that the only way they can prosper is to sell drugs and be lookouts on the corners of the streets?

Miracle in a Miracle

What happens to the dreams of dying children who are well dressed and have every toy and every convenience and every videotape and look like little Hollywood celebrities? These same children would give their life for a moment of true affection from their upward-climbing parents. What happens to the agendas of dying children?

The little girl issues can easily be trampled in the press of getting the promotion on the job, of having our own paycheck. The little girls' issues can get buried under the soil of our being so impressed with ourselves, getting a bigger house and a grander apartment, getting a passport and a visa, and flying around the world.

Just as abruptly as we forget about those that issue from our wombs, Mark diverts the readers' attention with equal abruptness in verse 25. The emphasis is directed from the dying child to the sick woman. With minimum transition, the scripture says, "And a woman was there."

Before young girls have time to understand their bodies, and be trained and disciplined in how to be a woman, life abruptly changes and thrusts them into a position of womanhood. So the issues of the dying girl are lost in the transition.

In verse 25, there is a woman, but I want you to know that wherever there has been a dying girl that has been forgotten, it will result in a sick woman. We may be able to dress her up. We may be able to fix it up. When there are dying girls whose needs have not been answered, we are going to find many sick women. Therefore, when we get to the 25th verse we see that things have changed.

We are not confused at all about the girl and the woman and that they are two separate characters. Nevertheless, we see a fusion of the two. There is a woman that was there who had been subjected to bleeding for twelve years. There is a dying girl who was how old? According to the other Gospels, she was twelve years old. So as long as this girl had been living, this woman has been hurting. As long as there are little girls who have never been able to tell anyone about the inappropriate touching or how they were left in the care of unscrupulous people, we will continue to have adults with unresolved issues.

The Word of God speaks to us naturally, but bless God, it also speaks to us spiritually. Dying girls make for sick women. As we move through the chapter, we see that this woman, who has been bleeding, with these unresolved issues in her life for twelve years, had suffered a great deal under the care of many doctors.

We have suffered under many, many doctors. So many people seem to have prescriptions for our lives. They want to tell us how to dress. They want to tell us how to live, and how to spend our money. They want to tell us how to talk and even how to worship. The Bible said she spent all she had.

We turn to the television to the shopping channel and we spend all we have trying to buy happiness and trying to buy pleasure and bowing at the feet of consumerism. We spend all we have, sending for tapes that say "Seven Ways to Raise Your Teenager" and "Fifteen Ways to Satisfy Your Mate" and "Twenty-five Ways to a Healthier and Happier, Skinnier You." How dare these so-called doctors try to prescribe for praying, saved, and sanctified women of God?

She had suffered, and we are suffering, because we believe the lie of the media. We are suffering, because they told us that when we begin to age and when we become elderly, we are useless. We have suffered, because they have told us that we should not have more than the so-called norm of children. We have suffered because they told us that we have not arrived unless we meet a certain status quo, fit in a certain dress size, and have a certain hair texture.

We have suffered at the hands of many, many doctors. We have suffered at the hands of economists that try to tell us what we can have and we cannot have as people of faith. We have suffered at the hands of politicians that tell us how to think. We have suffered at the hands of those that want to reform the social welfare system, when it is our babies that are going without food.

We have suffered from inadequate health systems and we are the ones that are suffering from the lack of prenatal care. We have suffered at the hands of legislatures from Washington to Sacramento. We have suffered from back-room analysis and overnight Johnny-come-lately prophets. We have suffered at the hands of Teach America programs that have taken eighteen and nineteen-year-old girls and sat them in the front of an urban, so-called inner city, low-income classroom and told them to teach our children. They do not know what to say to our children. They don't know what to do but call them incorrigible and call the police and lock them up.

We have suffered at the hands of people with a crab mentality that make us, in our churches and in our pulpits, clamor for title and position. We have suffered in pulpits that have become perverted. We have suffered at the hands of many doctors. We have suffered. We have settled for less than God's best for our lives, rather than looking for praying men of God. We have suffered, being pleased with the money our sons bring home, when we do not know where they got it. We have suffered. We have compromised and told our daughters, "Since there's no husband in your life, you need a male in your life at any cost." That is suffering at the hands of many doctors.

This woman spent all that she had, and, instead of getting better, she only grew worse. Our schools are worse. Our cities are worse. Our marriages are worse. Our relationships are worse. Our lifestyles are worse. Our Christian testimony is weaker. Instead of getting better, we have only grown worse.

However, the Word of God says that when she heard -- even if you are saved, you know you like words. You want your children to say, "Mother, I love you." You want those grown sons and daughters to call you on Mother's Day. You want those significant relatives and marital partners in your life to remember you with kind words.

We are sensitive to words. We like compliments. We know it lifts us at any age, sixty, seventy, or eighty, to say, "Mother, you look good. That is a nice hat you are wearing. Mother, I appreciate you." We know what other people will not give us; we ought to give it to ourselves. We ought always to build one another.

Words took Eve down. She was listening to wrong words from the wrong source, in isolation by herself. Those same words will take us down. However, we can get a word that will build us up. The Bible says that this sick woman, maybe inside of her there was a dying child, but when this sick woman heard about Jesus -- it makes all of the difference in the world when we begin to hear about Jesus and who He is.

She heard about Jesus. I do not know for sure what she heard. Maybe she heard that He is the lover of our soul. Maybe she heard that He is the Lion of the Tribe of Judah. Maybe she heard that He is the Bright and the Morning Star, Prince of Peace, and the Author and the Finisher of your faith, the Alpha and Omega. Maybe she heard He is the Altogether Lovely One. Maybe she heard that He is the Consolator.

I don't know what she heard about Jesus. Maybe she heard that He was a righteous and a true Judge. Maybe she just heard that He was the True Vine and the second Adam. Maybe she heard that He was a Rock and a descendant of David. Maybe she heard that He was the Lord of Hosts. On the other hand, maybe she felt like I do sometimes when I am by myself and she just heard He is Shiloh. He is everything to me, the Bishop of my soul.

This woman had spent everything she had, and her situation grew worse and worse. The difference was that she was willing to hear a word about Jesus. When the Word of God comes, faith is increased. That is why the Word says, "faith comes by hearing and hearing by the Word of God." That is why the writer of Hebrews, wrote "Now faith," not yesterday's faith, not tomorrow's faith but right-now faith; faith that's good for me in every situation. It is faith that is good for me in every hour. It is faith that works when I am single, or when I am divorced. Right-now faith is faith at fifteen, to live saved, and faith to continue to bless God at fifty. Right-now faith.

Now faith is what picks me up; what gets me started on my way. It makes me hold my head up even when I can hear the hounds of hell pursuing me, even when my enemies outnumber my friends, right-now faith. Right-now faith will see me through and carry me across to the other side.

Right-now faith will dry the tears from my eyes. Right-now faith will be bread when I am hungry, and an advocate for me in the courtroom. Right-now faith will cover me when I would be disgraced and keep my feet from falling. Right-now faith. Now faith is the substance of everything that the dying child on the inside had ever hoped for. Right-now faith is everything that the afflicted woman was looking for. Right-now faith is the substance of things hoped for and the sho-nuf, downright evidence of things not seen. This is not a gamble.

There is faith for the times when I am walking through the valley of the shadow of death. If I am facing the Walls of Jericho, it is right-now faith. If my meal barrel is empty, it is right-now faith. If my oil, like the widow woman, is depleted, it is right-now faith. If I am black, like Zipporah, and Miriam does not like me, it is still right-now faith. In the kitchen it works. In the nursery it works. In the laundry it works. On the freeway it works. Right now faith.

She heard the Word. She heard about Jesus. And Jesus is the Word. He died for women that are responsive to words. He is the Word, made flesh. Therefore, any time He comes in the room, any time He is around, everything that a woman needs to have good self-esteem and good self-confidence is there. He is the Word for us in the morning and in the evening. If the telephone never rings, and the card never comes in the mail; if the children forget to write, you have a Word.

There was something about this sick woman who had a dying child on the inside. The dying child on the inside symbolized unaddressed issues from the past. Maybe some things happened a long time ago that she buried on the other side of the lake. Maybe there were some things she thought she had gotten over and gotten delivered from. Jesus said, "You are going to cross back over again. We're going to take a look at your sickness today, but I'm going to deal with the death of the little girl on the inside."

She heard about Jesus. She must have heard that He went around with healing in His wings and He had words of wisdom. When she heard about Jesus, she did not come getting in His face talking about "I'm a liberated woman." She came like a little woman. She came like a daughter of Zion. She came up behind him. Now, I know you Bible scholars will tell me it was because she was ostracized; it was because she had an issue of blood and she was unclean.

She could have come trying to put the men in their places. Nevertheless, the Bible said she humbled herself and came behind Jesus. I don't know about you, but when I really want God to do something for me, I don't start telling Him how good I think I am, or how long I've been paying my tithes. I don't rehearse to Him and tell

Miracle in a Miracle

Him how I haven't missed a prayer meeting.
When I really want God to do something for me,
I humble myself and walk with God.

*Humble thyself and the Lord will draw near thee.
Humble thyself and His presence will cheer thee. He
will not walk with the proud or the scornful, humble
thyself and walk right along with God.*

She came up behind Jesus and when she
came behind Him, she was still in the crowd. All
of her other concerns were no longer important.
The dying girl's issue had already been
overlooked. However, she touched His cloak.
Now listen to her faith. In Mark, verse 28, the
woman thought, if I just touch his clothes I will
be healed. This suggests she had a mental image
of the action and its results. That's faith. She
hadn't been in fellowship or relationship with
anyone for a long time, because she was left out
and considered unclean in her society. She didn't
have any more value in that culture than a child
had, the Word of God said that she was then
ostracized.

Imagine you went in a store and saw a dress
you wanted and could not afford. In your mind,
you left wearing it. The Word of God said she
had a thought and her thoughts were thoughts of
faith. They were not thoughts of foolishness or
fantasy, but she was thinking on the Word of
God, not thinking on carnal things.

How dare she dream so big? This little
lowly, humble, woman that could not sit at the
table with poor folks, entertained the thought of

touching Jesus. As she touched Him – she said, "I will be healed." Not only would the sick woman be healed, but also the dying child could be healed, the miracle in the miracle. There were things that didn't get healed, even though we got in prayer lines. Perhaps healing resulted by releasing our faith and making a point of contact.

Those things I do not talk about, the dying-child issues I can't even testify to, the things I can't tell my prayer partner on the telephone. She said, "I will be healed if I can just touch Him." When she touched Him, immediately her bleeding was stopped. "Immediately her old cranky personality, her old funny ways, her jealousy, that's the bleeding of some of us. Some of us are bleeding and leaking because we were the middle child or because we were the last child or because we were the first child and we weren't happy with mother and daddy's attention, because we had to raise the other ones. We carry all of that stuff over to the house of God.

When they tried to get us to work in the church, we started bleeding with those issues from a long time ago. When the woman touched Jesus' garment, "Immediately her bleeding was stopped." The Bible says, she felt in her body that she was freed from her suffering.

Then, "at once," there's Mark again, with that immediacy. He said at once Jesus realized that somebody had made a connection with Him. It must have been like when He came all the way from heaven down; a touching of the divine and the earthly. It must have been what it was like to have all power in your hand and then be born of a woman in a lowly manger. The passage provides a picture of extremes coming together. The high touching the low, the down touching the up. There was something about that touch. He felt power go out of Him. When Jesus realized it, the Word turned around, spoke a word, and said, "Who touched Me?" "Who drew the Word from Me? Who took the Word of faith? Who took the testimony of who I am? Who is it that was able to make connection with heaven?"

The disciples began to criticize Him and said, "With all of these crowds, why would you have such petty issues? Why would you ask such a question, with all of these people pressing on you?"

Who would dare to still be concerned about our children in elementary school, with all the major agendas and headline news? Who is still concerned about the rate of infant mortality in this country? Who will make sure that the dying girls' issues do not get lost? This woman felt it. When you arrive at verse 33, it reads, "Then the woman, knowing," – she wasn't feeling anymore--"knowing what had happened to her, she came and fell at His feet;" she fell down trembling.

Jairus, when he saw Jesus, fell at His feet and began to plead. When the woman of God touched the Word of Healing, it says that she, too, fell at His feet with trembling fear. Who trembles? A child trembles. Who trembles? A small, humble one trembles; one in the face of someone that is greater. "Of such is the kingdom of heaven;" people that have a childlike concern.

God help me to keep a childlike agenda. Help me to keep a childlike attitude. Help me, oh God, to keep a childlike naiveté. Help me not to be caught up in persuasions and politics, but help me to be like the child for whom you said you would make an opening. She fell trembling with fear. And she told Him the whole truth. Sounds like a little child that has to 'fess up' Sounds like a little child that took the lollipop off the table. Sounds like the little child that went and got ice cream when you told them not to do so.

There's something humbling about this. She was trembling, and she told Him the whole truth. And Jesus spoke to her. The proper translation of this word is that He didn't just call her "daughter," but He said, "Daughter of God."

Little Girl, I'm not talking to the sick woman, but I'm talking to the dying girl. When we are adult and sophisticated and presume we are grown up, we miss out on true emotions like laughing and crying.

Do you remember how you used to laugh as a child? Come on, tell the truth. I used to laugh so, until my mother and father would say, "Stop, Girl. Stop it. Stop, Girl. Don't be skinning your lip back over your teeth like that." Because when you are a child, you are uninhibited. You just fall out laughing, but now that we are adults, we barely flash a smile. "There's something real and honest about how a child approaches life. It takes a childlike faith to believe in miracles. It takes a childlike faith, after the things that happened in your past, to believe that God can speak to the sick woman and address the inner issues of the dying child.

He directed his words to her inner child; what was left of her childlike nature. We have learned to distance ourselves from childhood. But in most of us, if we would be honest, we could go back to when we once sang "Skip To My Lou" and when we played Hokey Pokey. I know it doesn't sound like theology to you, but you can remember the days when you used to patty cake. Come on, there are some things that little girls do. There were days when we used to play Jacks, Pick up Sticks, and Hopscotch. Those were days when we were carefree. We could jump rope and then switch it up and Double-Dutch. There are some things that little girls do. They play house. They play dolls. They go in the kitchen and play mama and dress up in high heels. They're not inhibited They're not bound. They are not overloaded.

There is a miracle in the miracle. I want to address the woman's issues, but somebody needs that little girl released in them. Somebody really needs to be able to be healed of her dying, little-girl issues. Somebody needs to be able to say, "Our Father" and know that He is a Good Father.

Somebody needs that carefree, little-girl spirit before she was burdened down, before she was shackled, before she was taught how to hush up.

I don't know about you, but my family already knows me. And there's a time when I'm mother. There's a time when I want to be a good wife. There is a time when the child is at liberty. There is a time when I just want to go back and remember what Jesus has done for me. There is a time when I want to go back and remember how far He has brought me. There is a time when I don't want to be concerned about the light bill and my son's tuition. However, there is a time when I need the Lord to deal with my issues of significance and security.

When Jesus arrived at Jairus' house, He put the crying people out. We shouldn't care what we have to do to get doubt and unbelief out of the room. The wailers were there wailing. The moaners were moaning, and Jesus said, "Get all this commotion out of here."

He said, "I'm going to deal with the little girl now. I've addressed the woman's issue, but the real problem is the dying girl."

He called Peter, James, and John and took them into the girl's room with him.

It is a sad thing, but it is fashionable to be a frustrated, sick woman.

Because, when you really have the Lord dealing with your inner issues, you can't do that in a public place. When the dying girl really is addressed, when you come from death back to life, one does not need an audience of spectators. There are times you have to steal away with the Lord.

He dealt with the outer miracle, but there is a miracle in the miracle. There are two sides to every coin; two shores to every lake. Where there is a top there is a bottom. Where there is a left there is a right. Where there is up there is down. Where there is an outer you, there is an inner you. Where there is an outer miracle there is an inner miracle. Where there is a grown woman there's a little girl. Where there is a man of God there is still a boy in you who every now and then, wishes he could pick up a rock and just throw it through a window. You know better, but you just wish you could get away with some of the stuff you used to do.

The child is still in you. The child is not dead. Jesus went in the room, after having put the crowd out. He took the little girl by her hand and He said to her, "Little Girl, I say to you, get up." Little Girl, little hopscotch-playing girl, little free, little happy girl that you once were before you knew about being depressed, before you were prescribed medicine to get up and to put you to sleep. "Little Girl, get up."

An old game came back in my mind. I remember, when we sang, "Little Sally Walker, sitting in a saucer; rise, Sally, rise, wipe your weary eyes. Put your hand on your hip and let your backbone slip - ah, shake it to the east; ah, shake it to the west, ah, shake it to the very one that you love the best." Well, I have the sanctified version. Let the one that really loves and adores the Lord unashamedly come out. The woman you were before you were squeezed into a mold of what you had to be and who you had to be. Get up, Little Girl.

We did not know. I had not been to seminary then. I did not know there was a theology in saying, "Rise, Sally rise. wipe your weary eyes. Turn to the east, turn to the west, and then turn to Jesus, because He is the one that loves you the best." Jesus resurrected her, and said, "Now give her something to eat; nurture her and feed her."

There is an inner part of us that needs to be fed. We are caregivers. We are birthers. We are nurturers. We are burden bearers. We are intercessors for others. He knows that we, too, need to be fed. He knows when there is a dying girl inside of the sick woman.

You know, it is kind of "in" to be a little bit sick. Everybody says, "I'm burnt out. I have a mild depression." We just slap these clinical labels on ourselves. It is a sad thing, but it is fashionable to be a frustrated, sick woman. Remember you are a miracle inside and outside.

Thank God for a persevering hope that never dies; a hidden faith that acts like a power beneath the surface. Just as there is a literary link between the daughter and the woman, there should be a living link between the daughters of Zion.

These daughters overcome external barriers with a persevering strength of commitment, character, and courage. The mystery of this text, like the mystery of womanhood is never fully disclosed. However, as we celebrate sisterhood we add this cast of Biblical female characters to our contact list. We thank them for their spoken and unspoken words, but most of all for their depth of being. They model perseverance: the power beneath the surface.

Questions for Reflection

1. How often have you claimed a label of sickness without even thinking about it?

2. Get up, little girl. Have you fed, nurtured, and sought healing for the dying girl in you?

3. What about the children? Are we so busy that we are no longer concerned about raising the next generation?

4. Have you played lately? Have you let the little girl come out and play? Rise Sally Rise!

ABOUT THE AUTHOR

Dr. Cynthia Rembert James has been described as having "a transparent devoutness, coupled with a glaring scholarship." Dr. James seeks to model the absolute importance of godly consecrated study and preparation. She currently pastors in Oakland, California while also maintaining an active schedule of speaking engagements both nationally and internationally. She has been married 40 years and is the mother of three.

To order other products of Dr. Cynthia James contact:

CYNTHIA JAMES EVANGELISTIC MINISTRIES
P.O. Box 10858 • Oakland, California 94610
Email: mail@cynthiajames.org
Website: http://www.cynthiajames.org

NOTES

NOTES

NOTES

NOTES